If You'd Been There in Bible Times

Stephanie Jeffs

Illustrated by Jacqui Thomas

Abingdon Press

4

CONTENTS

If you'd been there when David fought Goliath, what would you have seen?

If you'd been there when Jesus shocked some Pharisees, what would you have seen?

If you'd been there when Jesus got angry, what would you have seen?

100618

DRY LAND AT LAST!

Noah pushed open the window. It had stopped raining and the ark was no longer floating.

Blue sky! Sunshine! Fresh air! He breathed in deeply. The animals turned to the light, blinking.

Noah took a raven and held it up to the window. The bird stretched its black wings and flew off into the sky. But the earth was still flooded.

Noah waited. After seven days he took a dove and set it free. It flew high into the air and disappeared from sight. But soon it came back. There was still nowhere to perch.

Seven more days passed and Noah sent out the dove again. This time it came back, carrying in its beak a new, green olive leaf.

"The water has gone down! Thanks be to God!" said Noah.

Seven days later, the dove flew out once more. This time it did not come back.

If you'd been there when the dove came back to the ark, what would you have seen?

NOAH

The Bible says that Noah was the only good man left in the world. He obeyed God's instructions to build the ark – a large boat – on dry land, far from the sea. He was told to take the animals inside before the flood began. Noah and his family were the only people who were saved.

THE ARK

God gave Noah precise instructions about how to build the ark. In modern measurements, it was about 123m long, 23m wide and 14m high. It had three decks, a door and a roof. It was not made to sail, but to float on the flood water.

PITCH

Noah coated the ark with pitch, a mineral which can be dug out of the ground. It is a sticky black liquid which is waterproof.

Noah's ark must have been a very smelly place to live in for all that time!

TOOLS

Noah would only have had very simple tools, such as an axe, a saw and a hammer.

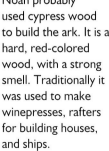

WOOD

Noah probably used cypress wood to build the ark. It is a hard, red-colored wood, with a strong smell. Traditionally it was used to make winepresses, rafters for building houses, and ships.

THE ANIMALS

God told Noah to take a male and female of every kind of living creature into the ark with him, so that each species of animal and reptile could be rescued from drowning in the flood. God also told Noah to prepare plenty of food to take with him.

THE FLOOD

This was God's drastic measure to make the world clean again. At first there was nothing unusual about the rain, but it didn't stop for forty days and nights. The rivers burst their banks, the seas flooded and underground springs overflowed until the earth was completely covered in water and everything in it was destroyed.

NOAH'S FAMILY

Noah had three sons. Their names were Ham, Shem and Japheth. Noah's wife and his three daughters-in-law also went with him in the ark. All of them were saved from the flood because Noah trusted God.

THE WORLD

When God first made the world it was a good place and God was pleased with it. But by the time of Noah it was full of violence and evil. The people on earth all fought with one another. They were unkind. They had all forgotten about God and how God wanted them to live.

THE RAINBOW

The ark landed on the top of a mountain. When Noah and his family eventually got out, they made a sacrifice to God to thank God for saving them. Then God put a rainbow in the sky, as a sign of God's promise that God would never flood the earth again.

FIND IT IN THE BIBLE: GENESIS 6:1 – 8:22

JOSEPH TESTS HIS BROTHERS

If you'd been there when Joseph's brothers came to Egypt, what would you have seen?

Joseph looked at his ten older brothers. He hadn't seen them for years, not since the day they had sold him as a slave. Now they stood before him, the governor of Egypt, trying to buy grain. They had no idea who they were talking to!

"Where are you from?" he asked them.

"The land of Canaan," they replied.

"Are you spies?" Joseph asked.

"No!" they said. He could tell they were worried. "We're starving and we've come to buy food. We're brothers! Our youngest brother is at home, and one of our brothers is dead."

"I don't believe you!" said Joseph. "Put them in prison!"

Three days later, Joseph ordered their release. "I will sell you some grain," he said, "but to prove to me that you are telling the truth, one of you will stay here in prison, while the rest return home. Then you must bring your youngest brother to me from Canaan, or the prisoner will die."

At last Joseph's dreams have come true! His brothers are bowing down to him.

EGYPT

The land of Egypt was rich and powerful. The River Nile usually flooded each year, making the crops grow and providing plenty of food for everyone. This year the floods had not come, and there were no new crops. But the Egyptians had been saving their grain for seven years.

JOSEPH

When Joseph was a teenager, his brothers had sold him as a slave and told their father that he had been killed by a wild animal. He had been taken to Egypt, where God had looked after him. Pharaoh, the king of Egypt, had made him the governor in charge of running the country.

CHARIOT AND CHAIN OF OFFICE

Joseph's brothers would not have recognized him because he was wearing Egyptian clothes. He probably wore a special chain to show that he was the governor, and drove a chariot.

INTERPRETER

Joseph used an interpreter to translate what his brothers were saying because he did not want them to know he recognized them and he wanted to see whether they had changed. In fact, he understood every word they said, and so he realized they were really sorry for what they had done to him.

SIMEON

Simeon was the brother left behind in Egypt while the others went home. Leaving their brother behind made the other brothers think about what they had done to Joseph all those years ago.

PYRAMIDS

The Egyptians used slaves to build huge pyramids, which were tombs for the Pharaohs. They also made other great buildings. The slaves had to make bricks out of straw and mud, baked in the hot sun.

THE BROTHERS

When there was a famine in their own land Joseph's brothers came to Egypt to buy food. They had no idea that they would meet Joseph there. When they found out who he was, all twelve brothers and their father, Jacob, were reunited. This is how the Israelites came to live in Egypt.

GRAIN

Some years before, God had helped Joseph interpret Pharaoh's dream about what would happen, and so Pharaoh had put him in charge of saving and storing huge amounts of grain in Egypt.

SLAVES

People were often sold as slaves by merchants, along with other ordinary goods. Joseph had been taken to Egypt by spice traders.

MONEY BAGS

The brothers had brought silver to pay for the grain. At that time, people used lumps of metal, measured by weight, rather than coins. The brothers had sold Joseph to the traders for twenty pieces of silver.

FIND IT IN THE BIBLE: GENESIS 42:1-24

9

SLAVES TAKE MIDNIGHT WALK TO FREEDOM

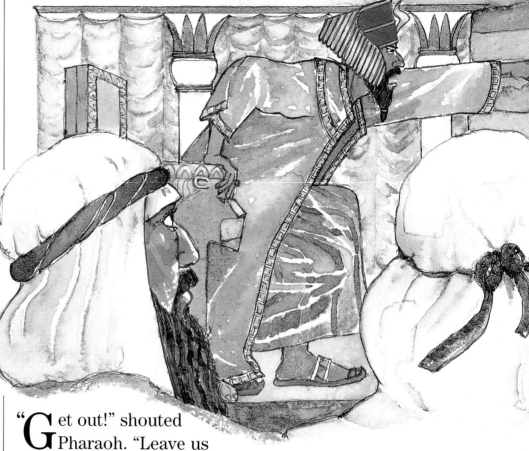

MOSES AND AARON

Moses had been chosen by God to be the Israelites' leader and his brother Aaron helped him. They had asked Pharaoh many times to let the Israelites leave Egypt, but until now he had always refused.

PHARAOH

Pharaoh, the king of Egypt, had agreed to let the Israelites leave Egypt a number of times before, but had then changed his mind. When his eldest son suddenly died during the night, and he heard about the deaths of all the first-born males in Egypt, he told the Israelites to leave.

"Get out!" shouted Pharaoh. "Leave us alone. Go and worship God – and take everything with you!"

All over Egypt could be heard the sound of weeping and mourning, as the Egyptians grieved for the loss of all their first-born sons and animals. Even Pharaoh's son had died in the plague. But none of the Israelites had been harmed.

"Hurry!" begged the Egyptians. "Leave Egypt, or else we

THE RIVER NILE

The greatest river in Egypt, the Nile, flooded each year, making the land very fertile and rich. When Moses was a baby, his mother had hidden him in a basket in the river to save him from being killed by the Egyptians. He had been found by an Egyptian princess and brought up in the royal palace.

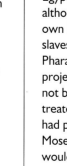

ISRAELITES

The Israelites had lived in Egypt for about 400 years, although it was not their own land. They had been slaves, making bricks for Pharaoh's building projects. They had not been well treated, but God had promised Moses that he would set them free and give them their own land.

MOSES' STAFF

God had given Moses special powers and he was able to do amazing things by using his staff, as a sign of God's power. Later, Moses held his staff over the Red Sea so that the waters divided, allowing the Israelites to walk safely across it.

will die too. And take whatever you want," they added, stuffing gold and silver into the hands of the Israelites.

And so Moses and all the Israelites set off. They had waited so long for the day when Pharaoh would set them free and let them leave.

By the light of the moon, a long procession of men, women and children carrying all their possessions and leading their flocks hurriedly left Egypt, giving thanks to God for setting them free.

> God led more than 600,000 men, plus their wives and children out of Egypt. God had kept the promise to make Abraham the father of a nation.

JEWELERY AND CLOTHING

The Egyptians were so keen for the Israelites to leave that they gave them gold and silver jewelery to take with them as well as clothes! These would have been useful to people who had very few possessions.

SHEEP AND CATTLE

The Israelites took flocks of sheep and goats and herds of cattle with them to provide milk and meat.

THE PLAGUES

Many times Moses had gone to Pharaoh and asked for his people to be released. Each time, God had shown his power by sending a plague; but each time Pharaoh had changed his mind and refused to let them go.

THE PASSOVER

The night when all the first-born males and animals in Egypt had died was the night God "passed over" the Israelites. The Israelites were told to have a special meal of roast lamb, bitter herbs and bread made without yeast. God told them to paint some of the lamb's blood on their doorposts, as a sign that he would pass over their houses and so protect their families from death. Each year after this, the Israelites celebrated the Passover to remember how God saved them from death.

FIND IT IN THE BIBLE: EXODUS 12:29-39

If you'd been there when God gave the law to Moses, what would you have seen?

ISRAELITES WORSHIP IDOLS

As Moses came down the mountain, he heard the sounds of singing and partying. What were his people doing?

He hurried down the mountainside, clutching the two stones God had given him. He could not believe what he saw.

The Israelites, God's people, were feasting and dancing and worshiping a golden calf. They had gone wild. They had forgotten about God and about Moses.

When he saw what the people were doing, Moses was furious. He threw the two special stones onto the ground, smashing them in pieces.

"How could you?" Moses asked his brother angrily.

"They told me to," replied Aaron. "You know what they're like."

THE MOUNTAIN

Moses went to speak with God on the top of Mount Sinai, while the Israelites waited below. The mountain was covered in cloud, which was a sign that God was there.

THE JOURNEY

The Israelites were on a journey to the land God had promised to give to them. They were crossing the desert lands between Egypt and Canaan and God had been showing them the way with a pillar of cloud during the day and a pillar of fire at night. They had camped at the foot of the mountain while Moses went up the mountain.

MOSES

Moses was old and wise, the great leader of the Israelites. God had given him the responsibility of leading his people out of slavery in Egypt and taking them to the promised land. Moses also taught the people about God.

THE TWO STONES

While Moses was talking with God on Mount Sinai, God gave him ten special laws or commandments which God wanted the people to follow. If the people kept God's commandments, God promised God would never leave them. These "ten commandments" were written down on the two stones which were broken when Moses threw then down. Later, God gave Moses two new stones.

The Israelites were God's chosen people. By making the golden calf they became like the nations around them, and broke God's second commandment.

GOLDEN CALF

Many of the different nations in those days worshiped statues of the bull-calf god, but God had forbidden the Israelites to worship idols. The Israelites had melted down their gold and jewelery to make a god like those worshiped by the Egyptians and the Canaanites.

IDOLS

An idol is a statue made of wood or stone or metal, which is worshiped as a god. God had already told the people that they must worship only God and not anything that was made by a human being. When the people nagged Aaron into making an idol to worship, they were being disobedient.

JEWELERY

Before they left Egypt, the Israelites were given gold jewelery by the Egyptians. Aaron asked the people to give their gold earrings to be melted down to make the golden calf.

ALTAR

An altar, made out of earth or stones, was a special place where the people burned sacrifices. For the Israelites, a sacrifice was a sign of praise and thanks to God.

THE ISRAELITES

God's people, the Israelites, had made a miraculous escape from slavery in Egypt. God had provided food and drink for them in the desert and had looked after them, and yet they had soon forgotten God.

AARON

Aaron was Moses' brother. He gave in to pressure from the people to make an idol, even though he knew it was wrong. Later, he and his sister Miriam complained about Moses' leadership, and were punished by God.

FIND IT IN THE BIBLE: EXODUS 32:1-24

13

If you'd been there when Deborah led the Israelite army, what would you have seen?

DEBORAH

Deborah was the leader of Israel. She believed that God could help them win the battle. She was greatly respected and Barak, the commander of the army, would not go into battle without her. Once the battle was won, she led the people in thanking God.

MOUNT TABOR

Deborah was standing on Mount Tabor, about 588m above sea level. This meant that she could see Sisera and the Canaanite army coming across the plain.

THE JUDGES

It was about 1200BC and during this time Israel was led by a series of "judges", one of whom was Deborah. These leaders had to help the people sort out disputes and keep the peace. The Israelites were not like other nations because they were not ruled by kings. God was their King.

DEFEAT FOR THE CANAANITES

"Go!" shouted Deborah. "God has already told us we will win this battle! Go and fight!"

Barak led the Israelite army down the hillside towards the Canaanites and their huge army of chariots. At the Kishon River the Canaanites were defeated.

Sisera, the Canaanite commander, knew he was finished. He jumped from his chariot and ran towards the tents of his friend, Heber the Kenite, seeking a place of safety.

Heber's wife, Jael, watched as Sisera ran towards her. "Come and hide in my tent," she said and led him inside. She gave him something to drink and then she covered him up.

"Keep guard," he begged, exhausted. He closed his eyes and went to sleep. But Jael was no friend of the Canaanites. When Sisera was fast asleep, she picked up a hammer and tent peg and killed him.

On that day Deborah, Barak and all the Israelites thanked God.

PROPHETS

At this time, God spoke to God's people through prophets. Their job was to listen carefully to God and pass on the message to the people. Deborah was a prophet as well as a judge.

THE CANAANITES

The Israelites had many enemies, including the Canaanites who had made life difficult for them for more than twenty years. The Canaanites were very cruel and had many weapons. When at last the Israelites asked God to help them, their Canaanite enemies were defeated and there was peace in Israel for the next forty years.

SISERA

Sisera was the Canaanite commander. As he ran from the battle, he was probably heading for Hazor, the home of King Jabin of Canaan. However, when Jael came out to meet him, he made the fatal mistake of going into her tent.

JAEL

Although her husband, Heber, was a friend of King Jabin of Canaan, Jael did not agree with him. She knew that Sisera would trust her, and because men were not allowed in women's tents, she let him think he was safely hidden.

> Sisera was killed by a woman, not by the army commander, Barak, because Barak did not trust God to give them victory.

TENT PEG

It was a woman's job to put up the tents, so Jael would have been used to using a tent peg and a hammer.

THE KISHON RIVER

The battle was won at the Kishon River, which was a dry river bed. However, it suddenly rained, causing a flash flood. The Canaanite chariots were stuck in the mud and their army was washed away.

CHARIOTS

The Canaanites thought they were unbeatable because they had 900 iron chariots.

FIND IT IN THE BIBLE: JUDGES 4:14-24

If you'd been there when Gideon defeated the Midianites, what would you have seen?

CONFUSION IN THE ENEMY CAMP

Just before midnight the Israelite army crept down the hillside to the Midianite camp in the valley below. Each of the soldiers carried a trumpet and a lighted torch, hidden inside a clay jar.

"Watch what I do, and be ready to shout," whispered Gideon as he divided his men into three groups.

The soldiers silently moved around the edge of the enemy camp and waited in the darkness. Everything was quiet.

Suddenly Gideon blew his trumpet and the silence of the night was shattered. Then all the Israelite soldiers blew their trumpets and smashed their jars on the ground so that the Midianite camp was surrounded by flaming torches.

"For the Lord and for Gideon!" shouted the Israelites.

GIDEON

Gideon was not confident by nature, but he was obedient to God. He trusted God to tell him what to do in order to beat the Midianites, and believed that God could win the battle for them. After this battle, Gideon became the leader of the Israelites.

THE MIDIANITES

The Midianites had attacked the Israelites for seven years before Gideon fought back. They were so cruel and powerful that the Israelites were forced to live in caves or in the hills and had to harvest their crops secretly to prevent the Midianites from stealing their grain.

THE ISRAELITE ARMY

At first Gideon had gathered an army of 32,000 men. God told Gideon that God wanted the Israelites to beat the Midianites by God's power and not their own strength. In the end the mighty Midianite army was defeated by an Israelite army of only 300 men.

TRUMPETS

The trumpet carried by each man was called a shofar, and was made from the horn of either a sheep or a goat.

TORCHES

The Israelite soldiers carried torches made from sticks wrapped in oil-soaked cloths. They set alight the torches, but hid them in clay jars. As soon as the jars were smashed, the torches burst into flames.

BATTLE-CRY!

Before the Israelites attacked, Gideon told his soldiers to shout, "For the Lord and for Gideon!" Because their battle-cry put God first and showed that they trusted him, they could be confident God would be on their side. The sudden noise must have frightened the sleeping Midianite soldiers.

Thousands of Midianite soldiers stumbled around in sleepy confusion. They grabbed their swords and some of them attacked each other in the darkness before fleeing for their lives.

Gideon and the Israelites gave thanks to God, for God had won the battle for them.

Gideon was not a brave warrior. But with God on his side, he could defeat a huge army!

CHANGING THE GUARD

Gideon and his army attacked the Midianites before midnight, at the beginning of the middle watch, just after the lookout guard had changed. The night was divided into three parts, and each part was called a "watch".

ARMY CAMP

The Midianite army camp was enormous. There were thousands of soldiers as well as a huge number of tents.

CAMELS

The Midianites lived in the desert and relied upon their camels for everyday transport, as well as in battle. There were thousands of camels in the Midianite camp.

FIND IT IN THE BIBLE: JUDGES 7:19-22

If you'd been there when Ruth gleaned the harvest, what would you have seen?

THE KINDNESS OF BOAZ

Boaz watched as his workers gathered in the harvest from his barley field. He caught sight of a young woman, working at a distance from the others. She was gleaning, picking up the leftover grain after the harvesters had finished. Boaz did not recognize her.

"Who's that?" he asked his foreman.

"That's Ruth," replied the foreman. "She's come from Moab with old Naomi. She asked if she could glean from this field. She's a hard worker. She's had only one short break all morning."

Boaz went across to Ruth. "Don't glean from anywhere else," he said. "Stay and work here. I have told my men to treat you well. And if you should need a drink, help yourself from the water jars."

Ruth was amazed. "Why are you being so kind to me?" she asked. "You don't know me."

"But I have heard all about you," said Boaz. "I have heard of your kindness to Naomi. May God also be kind to you."

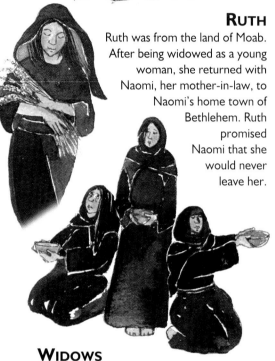

RUTH

Ruth was from the land of Moab. After being widowed as a young woman, she returned with Naomi, her mother-in-law, to Naomi's home town of Bethlehem. Ruth promised Naomi that she would never leave her.

WIDOWS

Life was very hard for a widow in Ruth's time because it was difficult for a woman to look after herself without a husband to provide for her. Widows were often very poor and had to depend on the kindness of other people.

BETHLEHEM

Bethlehem was a small town, not far from Jerusalem. Many years later it was known as "David's town", because King David was born there. Ruth and Boaz were David's great-grandparents.

SICKLES AND WINNOWING FORKS

The barley was cut with a sickle, a sharp knife with a curved blade and a wooden handle. When the barley sheaves were taken from the fields to the threshing floor, the barley was tossed into the air with a winnowing fork. The stalks blew away, while the grain fell to the ground.

Naomi had lost her husband, her two sons and her home. But Ruth stayed with her and looked after her.

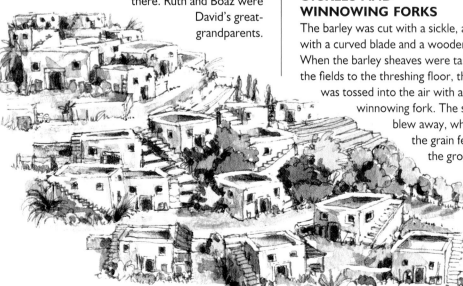

BARLEY

The barley crop did not take long to grow and could be sown on poor soil. The grain was used for making bread.

BOAZ

Boaz owned the barley fields in which Ruth gleaned and was a distant relative of Naomi's. Under Jewish law, the man most closely related to a widow was allowed to marry her, so that she would be looked after within the family.

WATER

To keep the water cool and fresh it was kept in large pots or jars. When Boaz told Ruth to help herself to water, he was giving her a special privilege.

GLEANERS

God's law made sure that poor people did not miss out at harvest time. The law said that the corners of the fields should not be harvested, but should be left for travelers or the poor. And if someone dropped some stalks while they were gathering in the harvest, they were not allowed to pick it up, but had to leave it for the poor to pick up. This was called "gleaning".

HARVEST

In Israel, the barley harvest was always gathered in the spring time, the first harvest of the year. The barley was cut and then tied into sheaves.

NAOMI

Years before, Naomi had gone with her husband and two sons to live in Moab, following a famine in Israel. While she was there her husband and sons died. Because she had no family in Moab, Naomi had decided to return to Bethlehem and Ruth went with her.

FIND IT IN THE BIBLE: RUTH 2:4-12   19

If you'd been there when David fought Goliath, what would you have seen?

BOY KILLS GIANT!

In the days when King Saul ruled Israel, the Israelites and the Philistines were constantly at war. The Philistines often invaded Israel, and this time they frightened the Israelites with a fierce, new champion fighter from Gath – Goliath.

Every morning and evening for forty days, Goliath stood before the Israelite army and challenged them.

"Who is brave enough to fight me?" he called. "Choose someone as your champion! Whoever wins the fight, wins the battle."

When David, an Israelite shepherd boy, offered to fight Goliath, everyone was amazed. But David was confident. He knew God was on his side.

"You may have all the armor and weapons in the world," he said, "but I fight in the name of the Lord Almighty, the God of Israel."

With one stone shot from his shepherd's sling, David hit Goliath between the eyes and killed him.

KING SAUL

The first king of Israel was a brave fighter but even he did not accept Goliath's challenge to fight. When David said he would fight Goliath, Saul was amazed. He offered him his sword and armor, but David found it too big and heavy, and decided to fight without it.

ISRAELITES

The Israelite army thought they did not stand a chance against Goliath. But they had forgotten that God had promised to give them the land.

DAVID

Only a shepherd boy, David had three brothers in King Saul's army. He had been sent by his father, Jesse, to take them food and to see how they were. He was sure that God would not let Goliath win. David later became a great king of Israel.

LIONS AND BEARS

A shepherd protected his flocks from wild animals. David had killed lions and bears many times; he was sure he could kill Goliath with a carefully aimed stone.

DAVID'S STAFF

David took a staff with him to fight Goliath. When he was looking after his sheep he would have used the staff to hook up any that fell down the hillside. Goliath thought that David was treating him like a dog when David came towards him with a stick.

PHILISTINES
The Philistines were a fierce fighting force, one of the Sea Peoples whose land bordered the Great Sea or Mediterranean. They wanted the land of Israel, and fought many battles to get control of it. They were sure that Goliath could defeat anyone. When they saw David kill Goliath, they ran away.

GOLIATH
The Philistine champion was 3.2m tall or "six cubits and a span". Human skeletons of that height which date from around this time have been discovered in Palestine.

SHIELD-BEARER
His job was to walk in front of Goliath and carry his shield, which was made of leather stretched over a wooden frame.

ARMOR
Goliath's bronze chain-mail breastplate weighed about 57kg. He also wore a bronze, feathered helmet, and greaves to protect his legs. He carried a bronze javelin and a spear with an iron tip.

> Goliath is enormous! He's more than twice as big as me and I'm 1.2m tall.

DAVID'S SLING
Goliath's armor was impressive, but it was no defense against David's sling. He selected five smooth stones and put them in his bag. Before Goliath could attack, he put a small stone in his sling, swung it in the air, let go of one end of it, and the stone hit Goliath's forehead. David's stone found the one place on Goliath's head not covered by metal.

GOLIATH'S SWORD
Goliath had come towards David without even drawing his sword. David took the sword from Goliath's own sheath, then cut off his head. Then all the Israelites saw that God kept promises when the people trusted God.

BRONZE AND IRON
The Philistines were expert blacksmiths and armed themselves with sharp, metal weapons, protected themselves with strong armor, and rode in chariots.

FIND IT IN THE BIBLE: 1 SAMUEL 17:1-58

If you'd been there when Solomon built the temple, what would you have seen?

KING SOLOMON

King Solomon was the son of Israel's greatest king, David. Solomon reigned over Israel about 950 years before Jesus was born. When Solomon became king, he asked God for the gift of wisdom. God was pleased with his request and made him the wisest and richest king of Israel. Solomon was able to use some of his wealth to build God's temple.

THE TEMPLE SITE

Solomon's father, King David, had wanted to build God a temple in Jerusalem, the capital city, so that the ark of the covenant would have a permanent place. David bought a plot of land for fifty shekels of silver, but God told David that he was not to build the temple and that his son Solomon would do so.

THE TEMPLE BUILDING

God gave Solomon specific instructions about the building of the temple. When it was finished it was about 27m long and 9m wide. It was destroyed by the Babylonians in 587BC, so no one is sure exactly what it looked like. It was built of stone and was probably the largest building in Israel at the time. Only priests were allowed to enter the temple.

SOLOMON FINISHES WHAT HIS FATHER BEGAN

"God's temple is finished!" said Solomon to the Israelite leaders. "All that remains is for the ark of the covenant to be brought to it. Everyone must be there to see it happen!"

INSIDE THE TEMPLE

The first room inside the temple was called the Holy Place where there were golden tables, lampstands and an altar on which to burn incense. An olive-wood door and a curtain made of crimson and purple cloth separated this room from the Most Holy Place. The walls of both rooms were made of cedarwood from Lebanon, covered in gold and decorated with trees, flowers and cherubim.

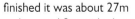

CHERUBIM

This is the plural of "cherub" and refers to the mythical golden-winged creatures which decorated the inside of the temple and the ark of the covenant. No one can be sure what they looked like, but it is thought that they were four-legged creatures with human faces and large outstretched wings. The Most Holy Place was "guarded" by two golden cherubim.

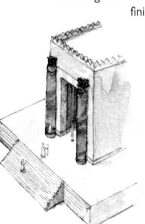

Thousands of Israelites gathered outside the magnificent temple. The priests carefully carried the ark up the steps and in through the doors to the Most Holy Place. Then they put it down beneath the golden wings of the cherubim.

Suddenly the whole temple was filled with cloud and everyone knew that God was there.

Then Solomon spoke. "Lord God," he said. "I have built this temple for you, so that you can be with us for ever."

He turned and faced the people. "God promised that I would build this temple. God keeps God's promises. There is no one else like God."

THE ALTAR AND THE SEA

Outside the temple was a large bronze altar to burn sacrifices, as well as some bronze basins. The largest basin was called a "Sea" and was used by the priests for washing. It could hold 12,000 gallons of water.

CRAFTSMEN

Solomon chose the best craftsmen to make and decorate the temple. Many of the craftsmen came from Lebanon or Phoenicia. Huram was an expert craftsman who made things out of bronze. He cast two highly decorated bronze pillars to go outside the temple. One of the pillars was called "Jachin" and the other "Boaz".

THE ARK OF THE COVENANT

This was a special wooden box, covered with gold, which contained the ten laws or commandments God gave to Moses. On top of the box were two golden cherubim. The ark of the covenant was the sign that God was with the people of Israel. It was kept in the Most Holy Place.

> It was a great day when the temple was built in Jerusalem. But Solomon knew that God was too great to live on earth.

CEDARWOOD

The cedarwood used in the temple building came from Lebanon. When the trees were cut down, they were lashed into rafts and floated by sea down to Israel. Cedarwood has a distinctive perfume and is very expensive.

STONE

Solomon employed 80,000 stone cutters to work in the hills round Jerusalem for the temple's foundations. He made sure that the stone was cut into the correct shape while it was at the quarry, so that the sound of hammer and chisel was never heard on the temple site.

FIND IT IN THE BIBLE: 1 KINGS 8:1-21

GOD SENDS FIRE!

If you'd been there when Elijah challenged the prophets of Baal, what would you have seen?

THE PEOPLE

The Israelites had been chosen by God to be God's special people. God had given them laws to live by written on tablets of stone. One of the ten commandments said, "You must worship only God, and not idols made of wood or stone."

THE WATER JARS

Elijah ordered water to be poured over his altar three times, using four large water jars. By the third time, not only was the altar and the sacrifice sodden, the trench was full of water.

ELIJAH

Elijah was a prophet, a man chosen by God to speak out God's message. He was one of the few people in Israel who continued to trust God when all the rest copied King Ahab and worshiped idols.

A huge crowd gathered on Mount Carmel. There was going to be a contest: King Ahab and 450 prophets of the god Baal on one side; God's prophet Elijah on the other.

"Who is real – Baal or the Lord God?" challenged Elijah.

"We will each build an altar and sacrifice a bull. Your

KING AHAB

The king of Israel was supposed to lead his people to worship God and keep God's laws. Ahab was one of Israel's most evil kings. Instead of marrying one of God's people, he married Jezebel, who encouraged him and his people to worship her gods, Baal and Asherah. Ahab blamed Elijah for bringing trouble to Israel, instead of realizing that Israel's troubles were due to his own wickedness.

BAAL

Baal was a Canaanite god, thought to rule the weather. A goddess called Asherah was thought to be his "wife". Queen Jezebel had 450 prophets or priests of Baal under her command, as well as 400 prophets of Asherah. People worshiped statues of these gods made of wood and iron.

prophets will pray to Baal; and I will pray to the Lord God. The true God is the one who answers by sending fire."

The prophets of Baal danced and shouted, "O Baal, send down fire!" but nothing happened. They danced and shouted until they were exhausted.

MOUNT CARMEL

Mount Carmel is the highest point of a range of hills overlooking what is now known as the Mediterranean Sea.

KING AHAB'S CHARIOT

Many kings had horse-drawn chariots, made of iron, which they drove into battle. After the defeat of the prophets of Baal, King Ahab traveled 27km back to his palace at Jezreel.

RAVENS

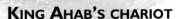

Being a prophet was a dangerous task. After Elijah told King Ahab that the drought would come, he went into hiding, for fear of his life. But God looked after Elijah. He sent ravens to feed him, and led Elijah to a water source. Later God provided a poor widow with enough flour and oil to make bread for her family and Elijah during the famine.

Elijah poured water on his altar and prayed, "Let the people know that you are the true God."

There was a great roar and a flash. A huge tongue of fire shot out of the sky and burned up everything on Elijah's altar.

The people fell to the ground in fear. "The Lord God is the living God!" they cried.

Elijah issued a brave challenge: decide who is the real God. Elijah's God did not let him down.

THE ALTAR

At this stage in history, most religions had a system of making sacrifices. The altar was usually made out of stone.

THE DROUGHT

God told Elijah that no rain would fall on the land of Israel until King Ahab turned away from idol worship. The drought lasted for nearly three years. The crops failed and most of the water dried up.

STONES

Ahab had allowed all God's altars to be broken, and had set up altars to idols. Elijah rebuilt God's altar, using twelve stones to represent the twelve tribes of Israel.

THE ONE TRUE GOD

For years, under the influence of bad kings, the Israelites had worshiped idols made of wood and stone. After the fire from heaven, a powerful sign from the great but invisible God, the Israelites were in no doubt: they would worship God.

THE SACRIFICE

Not all sacrifices involved killing. Sometimes incense was burned upon the altar. In this case, however, Elijah and the prophets of Baal each killed a bull to use as their sacrifice.

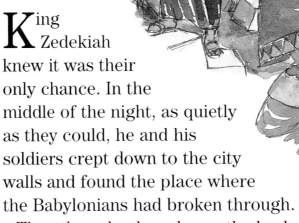

KING ZEDEKIAH

Ten years earlier, King Nebuchadnezzar of Babylon had appointed Zedekiah to be king of Judah, under his authority. But Zedekiah had rebelled, so Nebuchadnezzar invaded and besieged Jerusalem.

BABYLON

Babylon was the most powerful empire in the world at that time, and it ruled over a huge area of land. The capital city, Babylon, was about 1450km from Judah.

SIEGE

The Babylonians had surrounded the city of Jerusalem for more than eighteen months, and had attacked it. This meant that the people could not leave the city to get food, and so by now they were starving.

King Zedekiah knew it was their only chance. In the middle of the night, as quietly as they could, he and his soldiers crept down to the city walls and found the place where the Babylonians had broken through.

Then they clambered over the broken wall and ran away as fast as they could.

It was useless. As soon as the Babylonians realized the king and his army had escaped, they rushed after them and hunted them down. As the weak and weary Israelite army scattered in all

THE WALLS

Most cities were surrounded by thick walls and when an enemy approached, the city gates were shut. The Babylonian army had broken through Jerusalem's walls, which were double in places.

MIDDLE GATE

As soon as the Babylonian army had broken through the city walls, three Babylonian officials made their headquarters at the Middle Gate at the northern end of the city.

JERUSALEM DESTROYED!

LOOT AND PLUNDER

The Babylonians raided the city of Jerusalem, including the palace and the temple. Eventually all the temple furniture, which was made of bronze, gold or silver, was taken to Babylon. Even the two bronze pillars at the door were broken up and carried away.

directions, they left their king to fend for himself. The Babylonians found Zedekiah and took him to their king, Nebuchadnezzar. "Your sons will be killed and you and your people will be taken to Babylon as captives," said Nebuchadnezzar.

So the Babylonian army did as Nebuchadnezzar had ordered. They blinded Zedekiah and put him and his people in chains, and took them away.

Then they destroyed Jerusalem.

Zedekiah and his people had not followed God's ways. Because of their disobedience, God allowed the Babylonians to destroy Jerusalem.

DESTRUCTION OF JERUSALEM

Nebuchadnezzar made sure that very little of Jerusalem remained. The army broke down the city walls and set fire to the temple, the palace, and all the most important houses and buildings.

THE KING'S GARDEN

The king's garden was situated near the Pool of Siloam, Jerusalem's main water supply, at the southern end of the city.

CAPTIVES

When the Babylonians conquered a country they took everything of value, including the people. Anyone who was wealthy, clever, talented or useful was taken as a captive to live and work in Babylon.

THE PEOPLE LEFT BEHIND

Only the poorest people, who owned nothing, were left in Jerusalem. They were given the fields and vineyards to look after. This made sure that they were loyal to their conquerors.

FIND IT IN THE BIBLE: JEREMIAH 39:4-8

INTO THE FIRE!

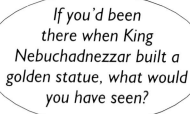

If you'd been there when King Nebuchadnezzar built a golden statue, what would you have seen?

THE GOLDEN STATUE
No one could fail to see this statue: it was over 27m high, nearly 3m wide and covered in gold.

The whole Babylonian nation stood on the vast Dura plain. Ahead of them, glinting in the sunlight, stood an enormous statue made of gold.

A herald walked forward. "You are here by order of King Nebuchadnezzar. When you hear music, everyone must bow down and worship this statue. Anyone who fails to obey will be punished. They will be burned alive in a furnace of fire!"

Suddenly a horn could be heard. It was followed by the zither and the lyre until the air was full

KING NEBUCHADNEZZAR
Nebuchadnezzar was rich and powerful. He ruled over the vast Babylonian empire and he expected everyone to obey him.

SHADRACH, MESHACH AND ABEDNEGO
When Nebuchadnezzar conquered Jerusalem, Shadrach, Meshach and Abednego were taken as captives to live in Babylon. They worked hard for Nebuchadnezzar and he put them in charge of some of his empire. However, they never forgot God, and chose to put God first instead of obeying the king.

BABYLONIAN GODS
Worshiping statues was part of Babylonian life. It was every king's duty to repair old statues and make new ones for the people to worship. Each statue represented a Babylonian god.

of music. Instantly the people fell to the ground and worshiped the statue. Everyone obeyed Nebuchadnezzar, except for three men.

"Shadrach, Meshach and Abednego have disobeyed your orders," reported some officials to the king.

Nebuchadnezzar was furious. "Then they shall be punished," he cried. "Throw them into the fire!"

HERALD
The herald was a very important member of the court. It was his job to make sure everyone heard and understood the king's orders.

MUSICAL INSTRUMENTS
Nebuchadnezzar ordered music to be played as a signal for the people to bow down to the statue. The lyre, harp and zither were all stringed instruments. The horn was like a trumpet, and the pipes and flute like a recorder.

Shadrach, Meshach and Abednego knew they had to obey their God whatever happened. They also knew God was able to save them.

THE FURNACE
The punishment for disobeying the king was to be thrown into a furnace. As the three men were thrown into the flames, the heat was so great that their guards were killed. But when Nebuchadnezzar looked into the furnace through a stoke hole, he saw that the three men were unharmed. Then Nebuchadnezzar understood that God had saved them and he had to admit that God's power was greater than his.

THE JEWS IN EXILE
From the time when Nebuchadnezzar invaded Judah and destroyed Jerusalem in 597BC, he took thousands of Jews to live in Babylon. They were free to live in their own towns and keep their own customs. Some of them became important government officials, but most of the Jews in Babylon wanted to return to their own country. About fifty years later, they were allowed to return to Jerusalem.

JEWISH RELIGION
Shadrach, Meshach and Abednego continued to worship God, even though they were far away from their own country. They wanted to obey God's laws, and one of the ten commandments forbade God's people to bow down and worship an idol or anything that had been made by a person.

FIND IT IN THE BIBLE: DANIEL 3:1-15

If you'd been there when Daniel was thrown into the lions' den, what would you have seen?

MAN SURVIVES NIGHT IN LIONS' DEN!

BABYLON

The great city of Babylon was full of magnificent buildings. It was traditionally thought that King Nebuchadnezzar had ordered the palace roof to be turned into gardens for his queen to enjoy. These "hanging gardens" of Babylon were thought to be famous throughout the known world at that time.

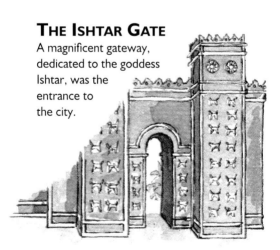

THE ISHTAR GATE

A magnificent gateway, dedicated to the goddess Ishtar, was the entrance to the city.

DANIEL

Daniel was one of the Jewish hostages taken from Jerusalem in 605BC by the Babylonians. He became a highly trusted and responsible administrator in Babylon.

KEEPING GOD'S LAWS

Although he lived for many years in Babylon, and he had been taught Babylonian ways, Daniel was faithful to God. He did not worship anyone or anything apart from God. He kept to the Jewish food laws and three times a day went to his room to pray. Like all the captives, he longed and prayed for the day when they could return to Jerusalem, God's city.

BABYLONIAN RELIGION

Magic and astrology and the worship of idols played a large part in the everyday lives of the Babylonians. Eating food that had been sacrificed to the gods Marduk and Ishtar was common.

King Darius couldn't sleep. He kept thinking about his old friend, Daniel. He must be dead by now, torn apart by the lions. And it was all the king's fault. He had been trapped.

If only he hadn't been persuaded to make that law. If only he'd realized. His advisers had wanted to get rid of Daniel, such a good, wise man. And now he was dead, mauled to bits in the lions' den.

At last it was daybreak. King Darius left his apartments, dreading what he might see and hear. Unless…

He went to the door of the pit.

"Daniel," he called. "Are you there?"

"O King, may you live for ever!" answered a voice. "God sent an angel to shut the lions' mouths. Because I am innocent, God has saved me."

Darius released Daniel and wrote to all the people throughout the empire of Babylon: "From now on, we must respect Daniel's God, for he is the living God who reigns for ever."

THE GOVERNORS

Darius appointed 120 governors to help rule his kingdom. Daniel was one of three men who had authority over them. Some of them did not like Daniel so they plotted to destroy him. The only way they could think of was to make him choose between obeying God and obeying the king. After their plan backfired, they were thrown to the lions themselves.

> I bet the king was relieved! Daniel's God must be really great.

THE LIONS

Lions were feared and respected animals, and roamed about the countryside. Kings hunted them for sport. Sometimes they were captured and kept for entertainment and executions.

THE SEALED ENTRANCE

Seals guarded the entrance to the den. Everyone who was of any importance had their own seal made by a jeweler. Darius and all his governors had signet rings and pressed their seals into lumps of clay at the entrance to the den. It would be obvious if anyone had tried to get in – or out!

DARIUS'S LAWS

King Darius was persuaded by some of his advisers to make a law saying that no one could worship anyone but him for thirty days. Once it was law, not even the king could break it! Daniel knew that God's law forbade God's people to worship anyone or anything but God.

KING DARIUS

Darius the Mede became ruler of Babylon after Belshazzar. Although he did not worship the true God, he respected him because he knew that Daniel was a good and honest man who was completely faithful to God.

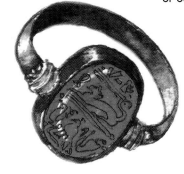

If you'd been there when Jesus was born, what would you have seen?

SHEPHERDS

In the time of Jesus, shepherds were uneducated people, and were not expected to see angels! A shepherd would never usually leave his sheep.

BETHLEHEM

This was the town, not far from Jerusalem, where Joseph's family came from. Mary and Joseph had made the journey from their home in Nazareth so that they could be registered for tax by the Roman authorities. Bethlehem was so full of visitors that there was nowhere to sleep.

INN

Bethlehem may have had only one inn. In those days, visitors stayed with relatives or in lodgings. Otherwise, like Mary and Joseph, they slept in the room with the animals in the lower part of the house, or in a lean-to shed beside it. Some people think the place where Jesus was born was a cave, cut out of the rock.

SHEPHERDS SEE ANGELS!

The shepherds could hardly believe what had happened to them that night. An angel had told them they were to go to Bethlehem to find the baby who would be God's Savior. Then the sky had been filled with the sound of angels praising God!

"Come on," said one, as soon as the sky was empty again. "Let's go and find this baby."

They ran down the hillside towards Bethlehem. They raced through the silent streets, looking everywhere for the place where the baby might be.

At last they found an inn, and a man and a young woman and a tiny baby wrapped in strips of cloth, lying in a manger.

DONKEY

Most people owned at least one donkey. They were used to carry people or their possessions.

OX

Cattle were kept for their milk and for meat. They were also kept to pull plows and carts, and the skins were used for leather.

MARY

While Mary was a teenager, and not yet married, she was visited by the angel Gabriel. Gabriel said that God had chosen her to be the mother of his Son, Jesus. Although Mary did not fully understand what this meant she told Gabriel that she was willing to do whatever God wanted.

JOSEPH

When Joseph, a carpenter from Nazareth, first found out that Mary was pregnant, he wanted to call off the engagement. But Joseph had a strange dream in which an angel told him that Jesus was God's Son and that he should go ahead and marry Mary.

"This is amazing!" they said. "An angel told us that we would find God's Savior lying in a manger. And here he is!"

As they left Mary, Joseph, and the baby, Jesus, they could hardly contain their excitement. They told everyone what they had seen.

That looks like a drafty place to put a new-born baby.

ROMAN SOLDIERS

Roman soldiers made sure that Emperor Augustus' orders were carried out, and that the crowds of visitors to Bethlehem remained peaceful.

MANGER

This was the animals' feeding trough and would have been filled with hay. It was not unusual to put a baby to sleep in a manger. People slept on the floor in badly lit rooms. A high-sided manger prevented the baby from being trodden on!

STRIPS OF CLOTH

Every new-born baby was wrapped up tightly in strips of cloth because people believed this made their limbs grow straight.

FIND IT IN THE BIBLE: LUKE 2:8-20

If you'd been there when wise men visited Jesus, what would you have seen?

JESUS, A LITTLE BOY

The wise men had a long journey and by the time they found Jesus, he was settled in a house in Bethlehem. He may have been anything up to two years old.

CAMELS

The wise men probably journeyed by camel, used by people for long-distance travel. Camels can travel for miles, even for days, with very little food and water.

WISE MEN

Tradition says there were three wise men and sometimes calls them kings. But the Bible does not tell us how many there were, only how many gifts they brought. They were probably highly-educated astrologers, possibly from Persia.

NEW KING? PALACE RUMORS

After months of traveling, the wise men arrived in Bethlehem. The star seemed to stop over a small house. Was this where they would find the baby King?

The wise men went into the house and humbly knelt down in front of the child on Mary's knee and gave him presents: gold, frankincense and myrrh.

Mary must have been surprised at such strange and generous gifts.

DAVID'S TOWN

This was another name for Bethlehem, because it was the place where King David, the great Israelite king, was born. About 400 years before Jesus was born, the prophet Micah foretold the birth of a great king in Bethlehem.

GOLD

Gold was the most precious metal in Bible times, and was a gift for a king. Even though Jesus was living in a very simple house in a very ordinary family, the wise men knew that he was God's chosen King.

Their last stop had been Jerusalem, at King Herod's palace. When they had told him they were looking for a baby, the King of the Jews, Herod had called in his advisors who had told them to go to Bethlehem.

Herod's last words rang in their ears: "If you find him, come and tell me. I should like to worship him too."

But after they had given their gifts to Jesus, the wise men went home a different way, after being warned in a dream not to tell Herod where the baby King was.

THE STAR

When the wise men first saw the star, hundreds of miles away in their own country, they knew it was very important. No one knows which star they actually saw: some people think that it was Halley's comet; others think it was a coming together of planets which occurred about this time; and others think it could have been a supernova, when a star suddenly becomes brighter.

THE HOUSE

After Jesus was born Mary and Joseph decided to stay in Bethlehem, rather than return to Nazareth. The wise men found them in a house, which was now their family home. Houses usually had one room, and the roof was also used for living space.

KING HEROD

Herod was not popular with the Jewish people. As he called himself "king of the Jews" he was very worried about the possible threat of a new king. When the wise men failed to return to him with news, he ordered that all baby boys born in Bethlehem aged two years and under should be killed.

JOSEPH'S DREAMS

Many people believed, like Joseph, that God used dreams to speak to them. Joseph took Mary and Jesus away from Bethlehem and into Egypt following a warning in a dream; so they were safe from Herod's evil intentions.

FRANKINCENSE

This sweet-smelling incense was burned in the temple as a gift to God, and a sign of prayer. It comes from the resin in the bark of the Boswellia tree in southern Arabia. It is very expensive!

MYRRH

Myrrh was also sweet-smelling and used as a medicine in Bible times. When someone died, oil was mixed with myrrh and the body was covered with it: this was called "anointing". Myrrh came from the resin of a thorny bush in Arabia.

If you'd been there when Jesus was missing, what would you have seen?

JERUSALEM

For Jews, Jerusalem was the holy city, a special place of pilgrimage. Mary, Joseph and Jesus, along with thousands of others, had been to Jerusalem to celebrate the great Passover Festival.

THE FEAST OF THE PASSOVER

Each year, in the spring, Jews remembered how God had rescued them from slavery in Egypt. They went to Jerusalem, where they ate a special meal, and made a sacrifice to God.

HEROD'S TEMPLE

The first temple in Jerusalem had been built by King Solomon hundreds of years before Jesus was born. It had been destroyed by the Babylonians and was rebuilt by Zerubbabel. King Herod built the third temple in Jerusalem.

BOY MISSING IN JERUSALEM

Mary and Joseph were frantic with worry. They had been looking for their son for three days. In fact, they had been on the way home to Nazareth before they had realized he was missing. And so they had returned to Jerusalem, anxiously searching among the crowds for Jesus.

At last they went to the temple.

THE TEMPLE COURTS

Parts of the temple were forbidden to ordinary people but the courts were open to everyone. This was the place to go to learn more about God.

THE YOUNG JESUS

At twelve years old Jesus was considered to be almost a man. At thirteen, Jewish boys had a special ceremony to show that they had moved from childhood to manhood. This trip to Jerusalem may have been to prepare Jesus for what was to happen in the coming year.

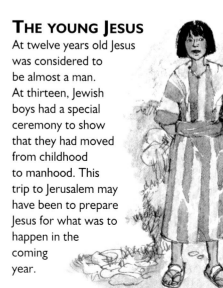

There, in the shade of the walls, they found him sitting with the Jewish teachers and experts, asking them questions and talking about God. The teachers were amazed at the things Jesus said.

Mary and Joseph rushed over to him. "Where have you been?" asked Mary. "How could you do this? We've been so worried about you."

"Didn't you know I'd be here, in my Father's house?" answered Jesus.

SCROLLS

These were like books, only they were made from long strips of papyrus or parchment, and rolled up from either end. Inside, they contained the law, which was written in long columns. As not many people could read or write, teachers were needed to explain what was written.

TRAVELERS

Traveling was often dangerous, so people traveled in groups or "caravans". Women and younger children traveled at the front, with the men and older boys at the back. Perhaps Mary and Joseph each thought Jesus was in the other group.

SCRIBES

Scribes were experts in Jewish law, which they knew by heart. They had lots of students to whom they explained the meaning of the law, and how to use it in everyday life.

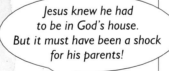

Jesus knew he had to be in God's house. But it must have been a shock for his parents!

PROVISIONS

The journey to Nazareth was 110km and took a number of days. The travelers would find water and buy food at villages on the way, but they also carried some with them.

MARY AND JOSEPH

Mary and Joseph would have made the journey from Nazareth to Jerusalem and back in the company of friends and relations from home. They were understandably upset when Jesus was missing. Although they knew that Jesus was God's Son, they didn't really understand when he talked about God as his Father.

TEACHERS

Jewish teachers or "rabbis" met in the temple courts to discuss the scriptures. At Passover time some of the greatest teachers would be there. Anyone could listen and ask questions. They were amazed at Jesus' knowledge and understanding.

If you'd been there when the fishermen let down their nets, what would you have seen?

FISHERMEN TOLD TO CATCH PEOPLE NOT FISH!

GALILEE

Galilee was a busy, prosperous Roman province to the west of a large freshwater lake, sometimes called the Sea of Galilee. Jesus spent a lot of time in this area, and many of his friends and followers lived and worked here.

FISH

Fishing was very important and brought lots of money to the region. There were more than twenty-five different types of fish in the Sea of Galilee.

DRYING AND SALTING

Because it was so plentiful, most people ate a lot of fresh fish. It was also dried in the sun or covered in a thick layer of salt to keep it from decaying.

Peter the fisherman liked this traveling teacher, Jesus. He liked the way crowds of people came to Jesus to hear about God. He liked the way Jesus asked to use his boat so that he could talk to the crowds on the shore.

So when Jesus told him to take the boat out further and let down the nets to catch some fish, he did what Jesus said,

NETS

Fishermen used drag-nets which had corks around the top edge of the net to help keep it afloat, and weights in the bottom to hold it down. When the net was full, the fisherman would pull a rope to close the net before hauling it on board. Keeping the nets in good condition was very important.

BOATS

Fishing boats were small and made of wood. They had to be rowed, although sometimes a sail was used. Most fishing was done at night.

even though he and Andrew had fished all night and caught nothing.

They rowed out and lowered their nets. Immediately the nets filled with fish. "Come and help us!" they shouted to James and John. Together they hauled in the nets, bursting with fish.

Peter looked at Jesus. It was incredible! He fell to his knees in fear and awe.

"Don't be afraid," said Jesus. "From now on, you'll all be catching people for God."

There must have been a huge number of fish! They nearly sank two fishing boats.

FOLLOWERS

There were many religious teachers at this time who had followers or "disciples". They were like students or pupils who would learn from their teacher and try to copy everything he did. Crowds followed Jesus everywhere he went.

JESUS' FIRST DISCIPLES

When Peter saw how many fish he had caught, he knew that it was a miracle. Jesus was such an amazing person that Peter and his brother Andrew left their jobs to follow him. Their friends, James and John, who were also fishermen, followed Jesus too. These four were Jesus' first disciples.

CAMEL CARAVAN

Because Galilee was such a busy place and many people lived there, it was a good trading center. It also had good Roman roads which made it easy for merchants to get to.

FISH SELLERS

Once the fish had been caught, they were sorted. Some of them were unsuitable to be sold, so these were thrown away. The fish to be sold were put in baskets.

JESUS' WORK

Jesus probably worked as a carpenter for some years, taught by his father Joseph. When he was about thirty, he began traveling around Galilee telling people that God cared about them and showing them how to live in a way that pleased God.

SALT

Salt was easily available from the shore of the Dead Sea, which was south of Galilee. However, only the inner layer of salt was useful as a preservative or as a flavoring.

FIND IT IN THE BIBLE: LUKE 5:1-11

"LOVE YOUR ENEMIES!" SAYS TEACHER

> *If you'd been there on a hillside in Galilee, what would you have seen?*

DISCIPLES

Jesus chose twelve men to be his special followers who would learn from him. Jesus was teaching them a new way to live. To be a disciple meant not only listening to Jesus' words, but doing what he said.

JESUS THE TEACHER

Jesus began to travel around Galilee when he was about thirty years old, teaching people about God. Like a rabbi, or religious teacher, when he sat down with his disciples it was a sign that he was going to teach them something important.

Jesus took his disciples up to the hills to tell them about God's new way to live.

"The people who are part of God's kingdom are those who know they need God's help. They are truly happy," said Jesus.

"You all know it's against the law to commit murder, but it's just as bad to be angry with someone, and to think angry thoughts about them. It's easy to love your friends, but now you must love your enemies!" said Jesus.

"And don't forget to share what you have with other people," said Jesus. "But don't boast about it."

By now a crowd had gathered. "Look at all these flowers," said Jesus. "They don't worry about anything because God takes care of them. So you don't need to worry; God will take care of you."

"When you pray," said Jesus, "you don't need to use special words. Just begin by saying, 'Our Father in heaven.'" The disciples were astonished. They had never heard anyone calling God their "Father" before.

> *The message Jesus taught must have seemed hard to put into practice. But Jesus said God himself would help them to live this way.*

THE CROWD

Some of Jesus' teaching was just for his special friends, but at other times he taught the crowds of people who followed him. He always welcomed anyone who came to him, especially children.

BEING ANGRY

Everyone knew God's law about murder. They felt good because they knew they hadn't broken it. But Jesus said that even being very angry with someone and thinking bad thoughts about them was wrong.

FLOWERS

Jesus used the wild flowers growing on the hillside as an example of the way in which God cares for all the things God has made. In the spring there were plenty of different flowers such as poppies, anemones and crocuses.

PRAYING

Jesus taught his disciples to speak to God in a new way. They could call God their Father, even though God is holy, and ask God to provide for and protect them as well as ask for God's forgiveness.

THE HILLS OF GALILEE

The Sea of Galilee was surrounded by steep hills, where some of the land was farmed. Jesus often went up to the hills to be with his disciples or to spend time alone praying.

LOVING YOUR ENEMIES

Jesus said it was wrong to try to get your own back. It was better to show love to someone who hates you, or willingly to give someone more than they ask for. Jesus knew that God loves everyone in this way, whether they love God or not.

SHARING

Some people made a big show of giving to the poor because they wanted to look good in front of other people. Jesus said his disciples should give to others regardless of whether anyone else knows about it!

FIND IT IN THE BIBLE: MATTHEW 5:1 – 6:15

If you'd been there when Jesus shocked some Pharisees, what would you have seen?

JESUS KEEPS BAD COMPANY

TAX COLLECTORS

The Romans employed local Jewish people to collect tax money for them. No one liked paying taxes to the Romans who were occupying their country, and they did not like tax collectors because they overcharged people and kept the extra money for themselves.

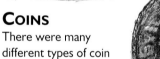

COINS

There were many different types of coin in circulation during Jesus' time. There were Roman coins, Greek money for the province, and local Jewish coins.

"Jesus is eating at Matthew's house!" someone said. They were shocked. Everyone knew what Matthew and his so-called friends were like – not at all respectable, and not to be trusted. Matthew the tax collector was a familiar figure in Capernaum – and now he had become a follower of Jesus.

Matthew had simply left his job and followed Jesus. Now he had invited Jesus and his disciples to his house

CAPERNAUM

Capernaum was on the shores of the Sea of Galilee. It was a very busy place, and a center for fishing and traders. It is the place where Jesus performed many of his miracles and taught people about God.

THE NEW DISCIPLE

Jesus chose Matthew to be one of his twelve special disciples who went everywhere with him. It was probably quite difficult for some of the others to accept that Matthew, a tax collector, had joined them. But from that day onwards, Matthew changed: he stopped cheating and lying and started to live in a way that pleased God.

FOOD AND DRINK

In many homes the food was very simple consisting of bread, fruit such as olives, figs, grapes, dates and vegetables such as beans and lentils. Wealthier people ate meat, and had a number of different courses in their meal. People mostly drank wine, as the water was not very clean.

OIL LAMPS

It was dark inside the house, so lamps were needed to give some light. These were made of pottery and filled with olive oil. The wick was made of rag or some flax was put in the spout.

PHARISEES

These very religious Jews were experts in God's law and thought they knew exactly how God wanted them to behave. They were horrified that Jesus, who claimed to know God, could spend time with people who were so bad.

SHARING A MEAL

However poor the family, guests were always welcome to share a meal, and were made to feel special. The evening meal was the most important because work had finished for the day.

for a party, with the other tax collectors and all those people whom nobody respectable would want to mix with. When the Pharisees heard what was going on, they came and asked Jesus' disciples, "Why do you follow a man who mixes with such bad people?" Jesus overheard the Pharisees.

"If you think you are healthy, you don't need a doctor!" Jesus said. "Only sick people need a doctor. I haven't come to be with people who think they are perfect. I have come to the people who know they need help."

Jesus was not afraid to do what was right. But the Pharisees made dangerous enemies...

FOLLOWERS OF JESUS

Although Jesus had twelve special disciples he had plenty of other followers, both men and women. Some just wanted to see what he would do or say. Others wanted to copy the way he lived. Many changed their way of life once they had met him.

SERVANTS

Matthew would have had servants to prepare and pass round the food. When Jesus said that God loved rich and poor people equally, people were shocked.

DINING

Matthew was probably quite rich and had a house with a separate dining room. The guests would have reclined, Roman-style, to eat their meal. It wasn't unusual for passers-by to look in at the window.

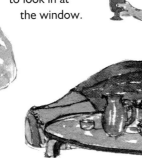

If you'd been there when a miracle happened at Bethesda, what would you have seen?

DISABLED MAN WALKS AGAIN!

O ne Sabbath day Jesus saw a man who had been unable to walk for a very long time. Every day he lay on his mat by the pool of Bethesda.

"Do you really want to get better?" Jesus asked him.

"Yes, I do!" replied the man. "But I haven't any friends to help me get into the water."

All round the pool were people who were sick or blind or unable to walk. When the water bubbled up, they were helped into the pool, hoping to be cured.

THE POOL OF BETHESDA

Bethesda, a large pool of water, was just north of the temple. It was surrounded by five colonnades or arched porches. This meant that people could be in the shade, away from the strong midday sun.

HEAD COVERINGS

To protect their heads and necks from the sun, most people wore a piece of material folded into a triangle and kept in place by a plaited hair band, made of wool.

UNDERGROUND SPRINGS

The brown colored water from the pools came from underground springs, which occasionally made the water bubble and move. Many people thought that the bubbling water was able to heal them.

Jesus must be very powerful – this man is walking again after 38 years!

SICK AND DISABLED PEOPLE

The doctors in Jesus' day were unable to cure many of the people who came to them for help. Many people who could not be cured found themselves outcasts, left to beg for money to feed themselves.

THE MAN WHO COULD NOT WALK

The man had been unable to walk for thirty-eight years. He had no hope of getting well until he met Jesus.

JERUSALEM

The city of Jerusalem and the temple area were surrounded by strong stone walls. There were a number of gates, such as the Fish Gate, the Horse Gate and the Water Gate. The Sheep Gate was near to the pool of Bethesda.

Jesus looked straight at the man. "Pick up your mat and walk!" he said. Without even thinking, the man leapt to his feet, picked up his mat and walked.

Some very religious people were watching. "Why are you carrying your mat?" they asked. "Don't you know it's the Sabbath?"

"The man who made me better told me to!" replied the man, as he walked off to the temple.

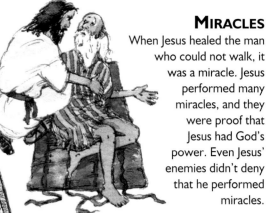

MIRACLES

When Jesus healed the man who could not walk, it was a miracle. Jesus performed many miracles, and they were proof that Jesus had God's power. Even Jesus' enemies didn't deny that he performed miracles.

BROKEN RULES

Religious Jews thought that carrying a mat was the same as working, and were angry that the man broke the law by carrying his mat on the Sabbath. They were much more concerned about the rules than they were about the man who could not walk.

THE SABBATH

On the seventh day of every week, Jews stopped work and worshiped God. It was one of God's commandments to keep the Sabbath as a special, "holy" day. This was a Saturday. Christians keep Sunday as a special day because Jesus rose from the dead on the first day of the week.

CROWDS

At that time, Jerusalem was very crowded because people had come to celebrate one of the great Jewish feasts. This meant that lots of people heard what had happened to the man who could not walk.

MAT

The mat was important to the man who could not walk. He could sit on it or lie on it. He might even be carried on it, like a stretcher. It would have been made with wool or linen cloth and padded with wool.

FRIENDS AND HELPERS

People who were ill needed friends or family to help them. There was no one else. The man who could not walk did not have anyone to help him until Jesus came along.

FIND IT IN THE BIBLE: JOHN 5:1-15

If you'd been there when Jesus got angry, what would you have seen?

THE TEMPLE

The temple building, restored by Herod, was the most important place in the life of the Jewish nation. It showed them that God was with them.

SACRIFICES

At certain times in the year, Jews worshiped God in a special way by making a sacrifice. This often involved killing an animal, such as a dove, or a sheep or goat.

DOVES

Poor people could not afford to sacrifice a sheep or a goat, so they could buy two doves or pigeons instead. These were sold in the temple courts, often at very high prices.

JESUS TURNS THINGS UPSIDE-DOWN

Suddenly Jesus grabbed a table and flung it upside-down, scattering coins everywhere. He overturned the traders' benches and stopped the merchants from carrying their goods. He drove out everyone who was buying and selling.

Jesus showed by his action that he cared deeply about God, but also about the people who were being cheated.

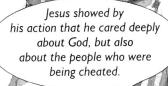

TEMPLE COINS

Because there were so many different coins in use, and people visited the temple from many different countries, everyone had to have their money changed to a special temple currency to buy animals and to pay the temple tax. The money-changers made huge profits by offering unfair rates of exchange.

THE COURT OF THE GENTILES

This huge courtyard was the one place in the temple where everyone – Jews, Gentiles (non-Jews), women and children – could go to worship God. It was not supposed to be used as a market place.

"Don't you know the scriptures?" he said. "'This will be a place of prayer for all the people of the world.' But you've made it into a place for thieves and robbers!"

The chief priests and teachers of the law heard what Jesus had done, and they hated him for it. "We must find a way to get rid of him," they said. But they were also afraid. The ordinary people loved him.

PILGRIMS AND VISITORS

Every Jewish adult male had to go to Jerusalem to celebrate Passover, so the city was very busy. People came from all over the Roman Empire to worship God in Jerusalem.

A PLACE OF PRAYER

Jesus reminded the people what the prophets Isaiah and Jeremiah had said hundreds of years before: that God's house was to be a place where anyone from any country in the world could come and pray to him.

ENEMIES OF JESUS

Jesus was not afraid to stand up to those who were doing wrong and to those who did not agree with him. The chief priests and teachers of the law did not like the fact that Jesus healed people, or broke the Sabbath laws. Not long after this they arrested him and sentenced him to death.

MERCHANTS

Passover was a good time for business because there were so many people in Jerusalem. Merchants would carry their goods on donkeys or camels, but instead of going around the outside of the temple, they took a short-cut through the Court of the Gentiles. Jesus stopped them doing this. The temple was supposed to be a holy, special place.

FIND IT IN THE BIBLE: MARK 11:15-18

If you'd been there at a house in Bethany, what would you have seen?

MONEY BAG

Jesus and his disciples needed money to live on as they traveled round teaching and healing the people. It was Judas' job to look after the money which he kept in a leather purse around his belt. Some of Jesus' followers gave him money to help him with his work.

JUDAS

Judas was not really concerned about the cost of the perfume. John, who wrote this down, says that Judas was in charge of the disciples' money, and often took some for himself. Later Judas betrayed Jesus for money.

BETHANY

This was a small village about 3km from Jerusalem and on the road to Jericho. Jesus often visited Bethany to see his friends.

WOMAN WIPES FEET WITH HAIR

Jesus was the guest of honor in Bethany, at the house of Mary, Martha and Lazarus.

Suddenly the meal was interrupted as Mary came to Jesus, carrying a bottle full of pure nard. She broke open the bottle and poured the expensive perfume on Jesus' feet. Then she bent down and wiped his feet with her hair. The lovely scent filled the room.

"What a waste!" said Judas Iscariot. Judas was one of Jesus' disciples, and it was his job to look after the money. "To buy that perfume would cost a year's wages. It could have been sold and the money given to the poor."

"Don't criticize her," said Jesus sharply. "There will always be poor people, but I won't always be here. This perfume is a sign of my coming death."

WINE CONTAINERS

Wine was kept in bags made out of animal skins. The skins would then be opened and the wine poured into pottery jugs for serving at the meal.

MARTHA

At this meal, Martha is serving the guests. Another time when Jesus visited Martha's house, she was too busy getting things ready to listen to him.

MARY

Mary used her perfume in a special way to show how much she loved and honored Jesus. It was also a sign of Jesus' coming death.

NARD

Nard was a perfume which came from India. Because it was so rare it was very expensive. Perfumes were usually kept in small pottery flasks, but expensive ones like this were often stored in a jar carved out of alabaster. The jar was broken open when the perfume, often used for burial customs, was needed.

Jesus knew that in a few short days he would be arrested and killed. Mary was preparing his body for burial.

THE GUEST OF HONOR

Guests of honor were treated in a special way. They were greeted with a kiss by their host, had their feet washed and were given special clothes to wear, or flowers to put in their beard or hair. They were given the best food and had the best place at the table. Perfume was poured on their head, face and beard.

EATING CUSTOMS

In some houses, people did not sit around the table, but reclined on mats or couches, Roman-style, propped up on their elbows. The men ate, while the women served.

LAZARUS

Many people knew Lazarus as "the man who came back from the dead". One day he had been very ill and had died before Jesus had reached the house. Jesus went to Lazarus's tomb and called to him. Lazarus emerged from his tomb, alive again.

FIND IT IN THE BIBLE: JOHN 12:1-11

If you'd been there the night before Jesus died, what would you have seen?

THE PASSOVER MEAL

A special meal of roast lamb, bread made without yeast, and bitter-tasting herbs was eaten at the Festival each year. This was to remind God's people of the meal eaten by the Israelites on their last night in Egypt, before God rescued them from slavery.

THE UPPER ROOM

Jesus and his friends ate their meal in an upper room. Lots of houses had large rooms upstairs. The food may have been provided by the person who owned the room.

THE FEAST OF UNLEAVENED BREAD

Although the Passover meal was eaten on one night, the Feast of Unleavened Bread took place for a whole week. During that time Jewish people removed all the yeast from their houses and made bread without yeast (unleavened bread), so that it didn't rise. This was to remind them that the Israelites left Egypt in such a hurry that they did not have time to let the dough rise.

It was the night of the Passover Festival. As they gathered round the table and began to eat, Jesus said, "One of you is going to betray me."

"I won't, will I?" asked his disciples, one after another.

"Will I betray you?" asked Judas, who had already thought about doing so.

"You said it," Jesus replied, as he ate from the same bowl as Judas. And Judas got up and left the room.

ONE BOWL

When people had a meal together, they often ate from one large bowl. They used their fingers, or dipped their bread into the bowl, using the bread as a spoon.

WINE

During the Passover meal, four cups of wine were drunk. Jesus used one of them to explain to his disciples that he had to die so that everyone could receive God's forgiveness. At the time, his disciples did not really understand what he was doing.

PETER

Peter was one of Jesus' closest friends. Before this meal, Peter rashly promised to die for Jesus. But Jesus warned Peter that before the next morning he would deny knowing Jesus three times.

WATERPOTS AND CUPS

Cups were made of pottery and were like small bowls. Water was kept in tall clay pots.

> I wonder how much Jesus' friends understood. Soon his body would be broken. His blood would be spilled.

Then Jesus stood up. He held the bread and broke it into pieces. "Take some and eat it," he said to his friends. "This is my body."

Jesus held the cup of wine. He thanked God for it. "All of you, drink some wine from this cup," he said. "This is my blood, the sign of a new promise that sins can be forgiven."

NO CHAIRS!

In Bible times, there were few chairs. People would sit on cushions or on mats. In the time of Jesus, many Jewish people had copied the Roman fashion of "reclining". This meant that the person ate nearly lying down, propped up on one elbow.

FOOT WASHING

Because the roads were hot and dusty, a servant would wash a guest's feet before he ate a meal. It was not a pleasant job! Earlier, Jesus shocked his disciples by washing their feet. He told them to follow his example and to serve other people in whatever way they could. He would have used a bowl, a jug and a towel.

THE BETRAYER

Judas Iscariot was in charge of their money. He was unhappy with some of the things Jesus said and did, and in the end betrayed him to the chief priests for thirty pieces of silver.

FIND IT IN THE BIBLE: MATTHEW 26:20-30

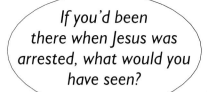

If you'd been there when Jesus was arrested, what would you have seen?

GETHSEMANE

Jesus and his friends often went to the Garden of Gethsemane, so Judas would know where to find Jesus. It was an olive grove not far from Jerusalem and near the Mount of Olives.

TORCHES

Torches were made by wrapping strips of material soaked in oil around a long pole, and then setting light to them.

THE MOON

The chief priests had had plenty of opportunities to arrest Jesus before, but they were afraid of the crowds who were his friends and followers. They made sure Jesus was arrested at night, so that no one else could interfere. It was the Passover, the time of the full moon.

JUDAS ISCARIOT

Judas was one of Jesus' twelve disciples, his special friends. He chose to betray Jesus by giving him a kiss, a sign of love and friendship. It was quite usual to greet another person by kissing them on the cheek. This kiss was also a sign that Judas was formally accusing Jesus of doing something wrong. This needed to happen if Jesus was to be tried in court.

ARREST

The Romans were not involved with Jesus' arrest at this stage. This was a religious arrest, ordered by the chief priests.

THE FATAL KISS

It was night in the Garden of Gethsemane. Jesus was there with some of his disciples. Suddenly a large crowd of people carrying clubs and swords entered the garden, looking for him. Judas Iscariot was with them. He walked up to Jesus.

"Teacher," he said, looking straight at him. Then he kissed Jesus.

It was the signal the crowd had been waiting for. They surged forward, grabbed Jesus and arrested him.

Jesus' friends panicked. One of them reached for a sword and swung out with it, striking the High Priest's servant on the side of his head, cutting off his ear.

"Put your sword away!" Jesus said. "My Father in heaven could send armies of angels to protect me. But what is happening now, must happen."

Then Jesus spoke to the mob.

"There's no need to use your swords. You could have arrested me before, but now is the right time."

His friends did not understand. They all ran away.

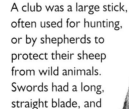

How terrible for Jesus to be let down by a close friend.

JESUS

Jesus did not resist his arrest. He knew that it would happen. Only a short while before, Jesus had been praying to God in agony because he knew what would happen. Jesus had told God that he would do whatever God wanted.

PETER, JAMES AND JOHN

Peter, James and John had been with Jesus while he was praying. Jesus had asked them to stay awake, but they kept falling asleep. The arrest surprised them and frightened them. James and the other disciples ran away, but Peter and John followed Jesus at a distance.

THE MOB

This angry crowd had been specially selected by the chief priests and teachers of the law, who were determined to have Jesus arrested.

HIGH PRIEST'S SERVANT

As Jesus was arrested, one of his disciples tried to defend himself. As a result, a servant was injured. In other Bible accounts the servant is called Malchus and the disciple is Peter. Jesus healed the servant's ear.

WEAPONS

A club was a large stick, often used for hunting, or by shepherds to protect their sheep from wild animals. Swords had a long, straight blade, and were carried in a sheath, which hung from a belt.

FIND IT IN THE BIBLE: MATTHEW 26:47-56

If you'd been there when Jesus was on trial, what would you have seen?

PILATE

Pilate was the Roman governor, and could have saved Jesus. But he was more afraid of the crowd than he was of condemning an innocent man to death.

THE CHIEF PRIESTS AND THE ELDERS

This was the moment they had been waiting for. Jesus had already been tried in the Jewish religious court and found guilty of blasphemy, but they needed Pilate, the Roman governor, to agree to their verdict to make sure that Jesus would die.

BARABBAS

A well-known bandit and murderer, Barabbas had led a rebellion against the Roman occupation. He escaped death when the crowd chose him to be freed instead of Jesus.

INNOCENT MAN FOUND GUILTY

Jesus stood before Pilate, the Roman governor. An angry crowd was gathering outside Pilate's house.

Pilate thought Jesus was innocent, so he went out and appealed to the crowd. "As is my custom at Passover, I can release a prisoner," he said. "Whom shall I free: Jesus, or the murderer Barabbas?"

Then he went inside and sat down. Suddenly a messenger rushed in. "Your wife says she has had the most terrible dream. She begs you not to have anything to

PASSOVER CUSTOM

Normally only the Roman Emperor could pardon a prisoner. Presumably Pilate had been given the power to do this once a year. This type of forgiveness was most unusual.

PILATE'S WIFE

Nothing much is known about Pilate's wife, Claudia Procula, except that she was clearly troubled by Jesus' arrest and trial. Her message warns her husband to be careful. She believed that Jesus was an innocent man.

do with Jesus. He is innocent."

But meanwhile the chief priests had been whispering among the crowd. "Release Barabbas!" they all cried. "Crucify Jesus!"

So Pilate went out again. He took some water and washed his hands in front of the crowd. "I am innocent," he said. "This is your responsibility!"

Pilate had Jesus flogged and then handed him over to be crucified.

ROMAN SOLDIERS
The Roman soldiers were there to keep the peace and to make sure that Pilate's orders were carried out. As soon as Jesus had been condemned to death, they took him away, beat him and mocked him.

CHAINS
Before coming to Pilate, Jesus was bound, which probably means he had chains put around his wrists, so that he could not escape. However, Jesus did not struggle from the time of his arrest.

PILATE'S HAND WASHING
By washing his hands, Pilate was using an ancient Jewish custom to show that he was not responsible for anything that happened to Jesus.

FLOGGING
Pilate had Jesus flogged before he handed him over to be crucified. This was part of the punishment, as it made the prisoner weak, and so death came more quickly.

The crowd must have been full of people whom Jesus had helped. He must have felt very sad.

THE CROWD
The chief priests and Jewish elders could not risk the crowd supporting Jesus. So they made sure that their own people were spread through the crowd, encouraging everyone to demand Jesus' crucifixion.

THE JUDGEMENT SEAT
While he was waiting to sentence Jesus, Pilate sat on a large, stone judgement seat.

FIND IT IN THE BIBLE: MATTHEW 27:11-26

55

> *If you'd been there when Jesus was crucified, what would you have seen?*

DEATH FOR THE "KING OF THE JEWS"

The Roman soldiers forced Jesus to carry his cross to the place called Golgotha. Then the soldiers nailed him to it, and hoisted Jesus up alongside two other prisoners, both of them thieves.

On Pilate's orders a sign was hung on the cross: Jesus of Nazareth, the King of the Jews. Meanwhile the soldiers took Jesus' clothes and shared them out, apart from his tunic which was made from a single piece of cloth. "Let's not rip it," they said. "Instead we'll see who wins it."

Some of Jesus' disciples and a group of women followers stood near the cross, watching Jesus.

As the hours passed, Jesus grew weaker. "I'm thirsty," he said, and someone fetched him a sponge soaked in vinegar, and held it up for him.

Suddenly Jesus cried out, "It is finished," and then he died.

THE CROSS
Being nailed to a cross was a terrible way to die, reserved for criminals. The condemned man carried the crossbar and was nailed to this, then hoisted up while it was attached to the upright post.

GOLGOTHA
This was the execution ground, outside the city walls of Jerusalem. It was also known as the "place of the skull" because of the strange rock formation.

THE KING OF THE JEWS
Pilate insisted that this sign was put above Jesus' cross, although the Jewish elders objected to it because they said it was blasphemy. It was written in three languages, Aramaic, Latin and Greek, so that everyone could understand it.

THE TWO THIEVES
Two convicted thieves were crucified with Jesus. One of them made fun of Jesus, but the other realized that Jesus did not deserve to die. Jesus promised this thief that he would be with him in paradise.

ROMAN SOLDIERS
The soldiers were in charge of the crucifixion and were allowed to take the clothes of the prisoners. Towards the end of the day they would often break the prisoners' legs to speed up death. But Jesus had already died when they came to check him. The soldier put a sword through his side.

SPONGE AND VINEGAR
Vinegar was very cheap wine. It was often given to crucifixion victims to help ease the pain. Jesus was offered a sponge soaked in vinegar and fixed to the stalk of a hyssop plant.

A DARK SKY
The Bible tells of many strange things that happened when Jesus died. One of them is that in the middle of the day it went very dark.

THE SABBATH LAW
Jesus was crucified on a Friday, and on Friday night at sunset the Jewish Sabbath began. It was against Jewish law to leave a body unburied overnight, and also against the law to do any type of work, so Jesus had to be buried before the Sabbath began.

Many of Jesus' friends had been with him for three years. None of them expected him to die in such a cruel and shocking way.

JESUS' MOTHER MARY
Mary was there when Jesus was crucified. Even though he was in terrible pain, Jesus was concerned for his mother. He asked one of his closest friends to look after Mary.

DICE
To decide who should have Jesus' clothes, the soldiers cast lots, or threw dice, for them.

If you'd been there when Jesus came back to life, what would you have seen?

DEAD MAN LIVES AGAIN!

Mary Magdalene was shocked. What had happened to Jesus' body? On Friday, after his cruel death, he had been buried hastily in the rock tomb, and the huge stone had been rolled across the entrance. Now, on the first day of the week, the tomb was empty. Jesus' friends, Peter and John, were approaching the garden.

THE GARDEN

The Jewish Sabbath lasted from sunset on Friday to sunset on Saturday. So Mary could not come to see Jesus until Sunday, the first day of the week. The garden where Jesus was buried probably had olive trees growing there, as well as sweet-scented herbs.

ROCK TOMBS

Joseph of Arimathea, a secret disciple, asked Pilate if he could bury Jesus. Most people were either buried in the ground or in rock tombs, which were painted white so that everyone knew what they were. Sometimes these tombs were caves. The tomb Joseph gave to Jesus was new, and had been cut out of rock.

THE STONE

A large, round, flat and very heavy stone was rolled in a groove across the entrance of the tomb. This way it was kept safely shut so that the body could not be disturbed.

BURIAL CUSTOMS

When Joseph of Arimathea and Nicodemus took Jesus' body down from the cross they would have washed it and then covered it with spices and wrapped the body in strips of cloth. Because of the Sabbath they were not able to complete the job, and so Mary came with more spices as soon as the Sabbath was over.

MARY MAGDALENE

Mary was grief-stricken when she thought Jesus' body had been taken. However as soon as she saw Jesus she knew he was alive. Jesus entrusted Mary with the important job of telling the other disciples that he had risen from the dead.

WITNESSES

Although Mary told Peter and John that Jesus' body was missing, they had to see the empty tomb for themselves. It was only after they had seen it that they began to work out what had happened. Later, Jesus appeared to all the disciples except Judas Iscariot.

Jesus had told his friends he would rise from the dead. But they were still surprised when it happened!

"They have taken Jesus' body!" Mary told them. The two men ran to the tomb and looked inside: Jesus' body was not there, but his grave clothes were. They ran back to Jerusalem, uncertain of what had happened. But Mary remained in the garden, crying.

"Mary," said a voice. At first, she thought it was the gardener, but then she recognized him. It was Jesus! He was alive! He told her to go and tell his friends.

Mary ran back to the city. "I have seen Jesus!" she shouted.

THE RISEN JESUS

Jesus had a "resurrection" body. He was able to show Thomas the nail marks in his wrists and ankles where he was crucified, and he ate with his disciples on several occasions after his resurrection. But he was also able to walk through walls and appear and disappear with his new body. He had died and been brought back to life by God. For Christian disciples everywhere, it gives assurance that after death will come new life.

SPICES

Jesus' body was covered with a mixture of myrrh and aloes to help preserve it. Myrrh had been given to Jesus by wise men who visited him when he was a baby. Aloes came from a common plant which grew wild in the area.

EMPTY GRAVE CLOTHES

Although Jesus' body had gone, the grave clothes were left neatly folded.

FIND IT IN THE BIBLE: JOHN 20:1-18

INDEX

LINCOLN CHRISTIAN COLLEGE AND SEMINARY

Published in the United States of America by
Abingdon Press, 201 Eighth Avenue South,
Nashville, Tennessee 37202
ISBN 0-687-01507-3

First edition 2000

Published in the UK by Scripture Union
Copyright © 2000 AD Publishing Services Ltd
I Churchgates, The Wilderness,
Berkhamsted, Herts HP4 2UB, England
Illustrations copyright © 2000 Jacqui Thomas

Printed in Hong Kong